McGrath Math

TEDDY BEAR
PATTERNS

Barbara Barbieri McGrath
Illustrated by **Tim Nihoff**

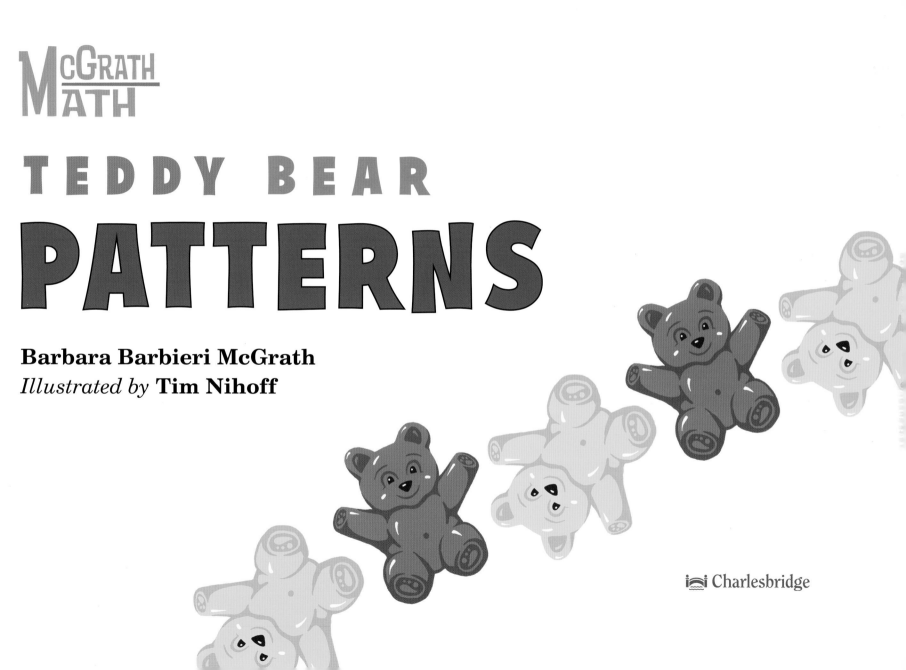

Charlesbridge

With love for Elizabeth H.—B. B. M.

To my warm, bright family of snowflakes,
each one-of-a-kind in pattern. X+O+X+O+X—T. N.

Text copyright © 2013 by Barbara Barbieri McGrath
Illustrations copyright © 2013 by Tim Nihoff
All rights reserved, including the right of reproduction in
whole or in part in any form. Charlesbridge and colophon are
registered trademarks of Charlesbridge Publishing, Inc.

Published by Charlesbridge
85 Main Street, Watertown, MA 02472
(617) 926-0329 • www.charlesbridge.com

Library of Congress Cataloging-in-Publication Data
McGrath, Barbara Barbieri, 1954–
    Teddy bear patterns / Barbara Barbieri McGrath;
illustrated by Tim Nihoff.
        p. cm.
    ISBN 978-1-58089-422-7 (reinforced for library use)
    ISBN 978-1-58089-423-4 (softcover)
1. Pattern perception—Juvenile literature. 2. Colors—
Juvenile literature. I. Nihoff, Tim, ill. II. Title.
BF294.M34 2013
516'.15—dc23   2012001340

Printed in China
(hc) 10 9 8 7 6 5 4 3 2 1
(sc) 10 9 8 7 6 5 4 3 2 1

Illustrations hand drawn digitally and collaged with
    found objects in Adobe Photoshop
Display type set in Animated Gothic, text type set in Century
    Schoolbook, and equations type set in Billy by Sparky Type
Color separations by KHL Chroma Graphics, Singapore
Manufactured by Regent Publishing Services, Hong Kong
Printed September 2012 in Shenzhen, Guangdong, China
Production supervision by Brian G. Walker
Designed by Whitney Leader-Picone

To make color patterns
let all the bears out.
Teddies will help us
bring order about.

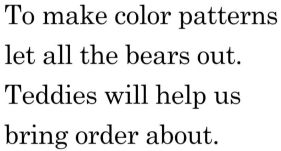

Sort teddies by color:
red, purple, and blue.
Group yellow and orange
and green teddies, too.

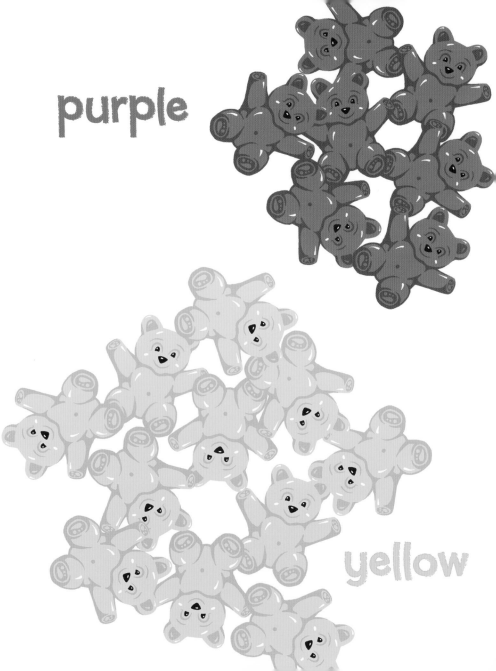

purple

red

yellow

Count all the colors.
Can you find six?
Let's make a pattern
out of this mix.

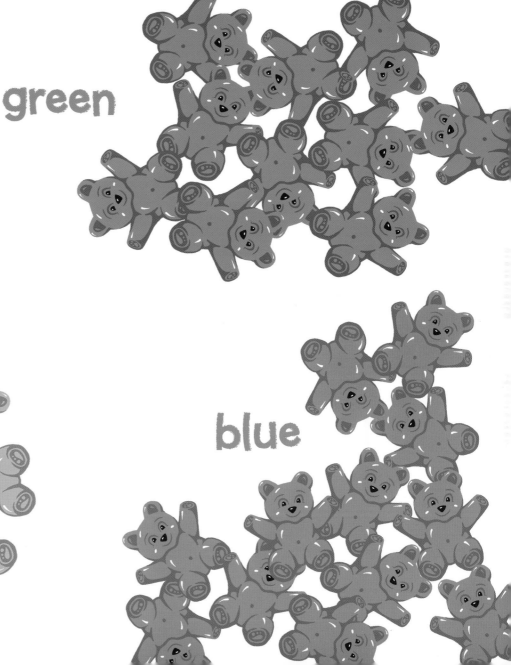

green

orange

blue

Making patterns is easy
with two colors of bears.
Line them up neatly
in two-color pairs.

Wiggle a green bear
between each red and yellow.
Say, "Excuse me, red guy!
Thanks, yellow fellow!"

Now put a purple bear
to the right of each green.

They're cutting the line
(but not to be mean).

Orange and blue bears
soon join the parade.
The line got so long—
just look what you made!

Six colors in order:
Wow! What a sight!
Try saying the pattern
from the left to the right.

This parade could keep going—
wouldn't that be a treat?
What's fun about patterns
is they always repeat.

Now try this pattern.

It's easy to do.

Yellow, yellow, blue.

Yellow, yellow, blue.

$$\begin{array}{r} 6 \\ + 6 \\ \hline 12 \end{array}$$

Start a new pattern
on the next line.
Purple, purple, red.
Then again: one more time.

That's twelve little bears.
Plus six more is eighteen.
Orange, orange, green.
Orange, orange, green.

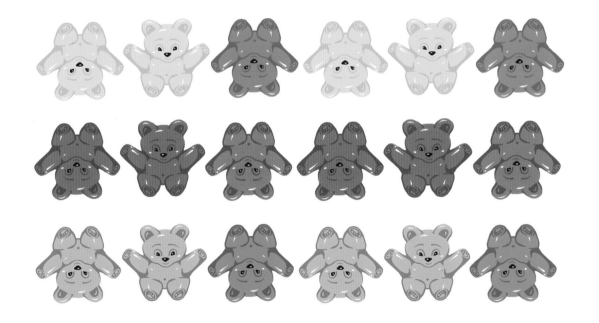

6
6
+ 6
‾‾‾‾
18

Use the three lines
of bears that you see
to answer this question:
What's six teddies times three?

6 x 3 = 18

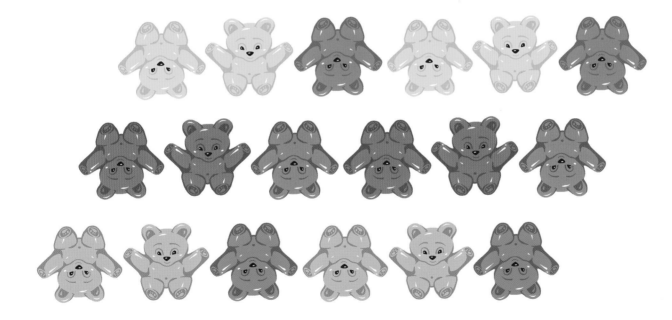

Take away the two bears
that are first in each row.
Two yellow, two purple,
two orange can go.

Look up and look down.

By moving just three,

patterns appear.

(I think you'll agree.)

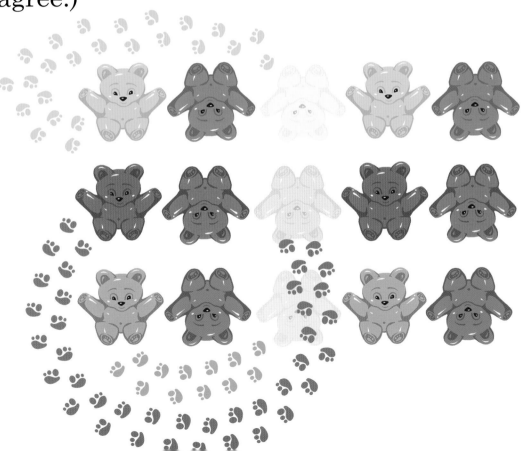

Let's make a pattern
that's totally new.
Place the teddies by color,
arranged two by two.

2

4

6

Can you use the bears
to count to twelve by twos?
The pattern makes it easy.
The colors give you clues.

8   10   12

Now put the bears like this.
Here's a fun new way to count.

Skip-count teddies by two
to get the total amount.

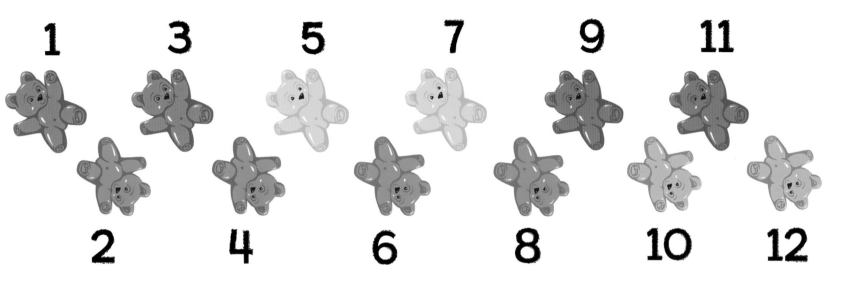

1 3 5 7 9 11
2 4 6 8 10 12

Do you see what they see?
If you do please give a nod.
The bottom bears are even;
the top bears are odd.

Design a bear pattern
for this page in the book.

Try again! Use all the colors.
How do they look?

It's OK if your patterns
are different from these.
A pattern can repeat
any way that you please.

Now make a big circle.
Fit all the bears in.
Find any three places
where the pattern begins.

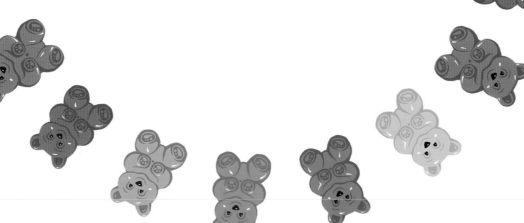

Patterns can come
in all shapes and sizes.

They can be silly
and full of surprises.

It's a bear pattern party!
There's no need to wait.
You finished this book.
Now bears celebrate!

Let's relax and review. You deserve a nice rest.
Take a big teddy bow because you did your best!

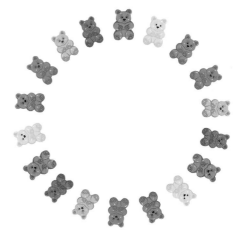

SORTING BY COLOR

Red   Purple   Yellow   Orange   Green   Blue

COLOR PATTERNS

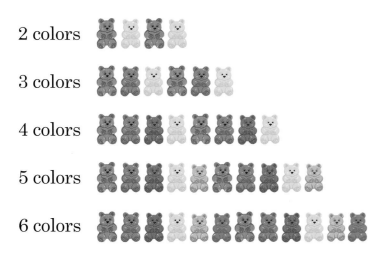

2 colors

3 colors

4 colors

5 colors

6 colors

SKIP-COUNTING
ODD AND EVEN NUMBERS

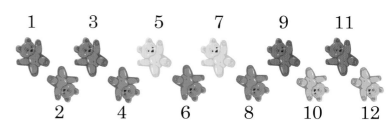

1   3   5   7   9   11

2   4   6   8   10   12

IDENTIFYING PATTERNS